# Copyright



By JUDITH INNOCENT

# Table of contents

## 28 DAYS OF DAILY DEVOTIONALS

*BEING COMMENDED BY GOD
*STANDING FAST IN HIM
*THE BENEFITS OF SERVICE
*THEIR WORKS DO FOLLOW THEM
*THE BAPTISM OF HIS SUFFERING
*OBTAINING THE CROWN OF RIGHTEOUSNESS
*RECEIVING STRENGTH ON THE MOUNTAIN OF FAMILY
*THE SHEPHERD'S CROWN
*BEING BOLD ON THE DAY OF JUDGMENT
* COMMUNICATION IN MARRIAGE
* REIGNING WITH HIM IN ETERNITY
*HOW TO CHOOSE RIGHT
*PARENTING ACCORDING TO THE SCRIPTURES

*THE FAMILY THAT PRAYS TOGETHER STAYS TOGETHER
*ARE YOU A FRIEND OR ARE YOU BEING FRIENDLY?

*THE IMPORTANCE OF FAITHFULNESS IN RELATIONSHIPS
*ISOLATION BEFORE DESTRUCTION
*THE POWER OF AGREEMENT
*THE BIBLICAL VIEW ON PREMARITAL SEX
*THE ADMINISTRATIVE MINISTRY
*THE PURPOSE AND POWER OF FORGIVENESS
*BUILDING HIS CHURCH USING HIS METHODS
*LOVE FOR THE BROTHERHOOD
*THE POWER OF THE ENVIRONMENT
*THE PURPOSE AND POWER OF SMALL GROUPS
*THE MAKING OF THE MAN GOD USES
*THE VALUE OF SPIRIT CONTROLLED EMOTIONS
*PRAY TO THE LORD OF THE HARVEST

## INTRODUCTION

This book is a straightforward manual for your daily devotions as a church, family, group of coworkers, or simply a group of friends that pray together. Go over the Bible verses and prayers.

We can be completely sculpted by the Potter after being burned by hardship.

Jeremiah 18:1-6, read.

The vessel had damage. . . It seemed appropriate to the potter to make, so he turned it into another vessel. In Jeremiah 18:4,

When the love and grace of God are applied, a broken life can be restored. When the prophet Jeremiah observed a potter at work, he observed that whenever an object was ruined, the potter simply remade it, according to what is recorded in the Old

Testament (Jer. 18:1-6). God said that the ancient Israelites were like clay in His hands.

# Chapter 1

Day 1: DAILY DEVOTIONALS
BEING COMMENDED OF GOD.
Some worthy saints served and exalted the Lamb while they lived on the planet. This suggests that having Heaven as your final goal and being born again are not sufficient. We have been given Gifts, and with these Gifts, we have been given Assignments to complete to carry out the Father's Will on Earth.

Several synonyms for faithfulness include dependability, loyalty, reliability, trustworthiness, and fidelity. Faithfulness may be described as "the trait of remaining constant in attachment or commitment." The Bible made this reality quite clear:

"Cursed is he who does not fully serve the Lord. Therefore, an unfaithful person in this context does not do so.

Notice that the problem in the Scripture is not whose work is done, but rather the attitude of dishonesty or infidelity with which it is done: "Does the Work of the Lord deceitfully; and cursed is he who withholds his sword from blood.

The onus is on us to earn God's Trust because *"Depending on an unreliable man in a crisis is like trying to chew with a loose tooth or walk with a crippled foot."* Proverbs 17:19. The Lord God Almighty places an extremely high premium on the incomparable virtue of faithfulness even at the expense of competence. Proverbs 17:19.

The Lord God Almighty places an extremely high premium on the incomparable virtue of faithfulness even at the expense of competence. 25:19(GNT). The Lord grants us the Grace to remain faithful to Him always.

Remember that stewardship is managing another man's estate in the best interest of the owner. The life we have, and the resources and abilities that were given to us are opportunities for stewardship. Everyone's work or stewardship will be evaluated for commendation or condemnation.

If our work is commended, our scope of stewardship will be increased with more resources and authority. *(Lk. 19:12-27; Matt. 25:14-30)* A heartfelt commendation from a parent or superior is like an energizer and affirmation of trust and confidence in the recipients' potential.

As we journey through life, whatever form of resources God has bestowed upon us will certainly be accounted for. Will you be among those that will hear, "WELL DONE good (competent, fruitful) and faithful servant" or "you WICKED and SLOTHFUL servant?" Do not forget that the Master of stewards brought those that did well into the joy of their Master. They became both shareholders and stakeholders in their Master's Estate.

*PRAYER:*
Father, thank You for counting us worthy to be made stewards. Lord, please help us to always remember the reasons for which we are witnesses and enable us to always live and act by Your Standards.

Give us the Grace to always work with sincerity of heart so we would receive Your Commendation as faithful and fruitful stewards in Jesus' Name. Amen.

# Chapter 2

*Day 2: DAILY DEVOTIONAL*
*STANDING FAST IN HIM.*

BIBLE READING: EPHESIANS 6:10-17; 2CORINTHIANS 12:9-10; 1CORINTHIANS 16:13; JUDE 1:24*

"For we do not wrestle against flesh and blood, but principalities, against powers, against the rulers of the darkness of this age, against spiritual hosts of wickedness in the Heavenly places. Therefore, take up the Whole Armour of God, that you may be able to withstand in the evil day, and having done all, to stand." Ephesians 6:12-13(NKJV)*

We must never forget that we have unseen enemies whose number one desire and assignment is to stop us from getting our Inheritance. By Inheritance, we do not refer to mundane things like material possessions. The Major Inheritance the enemy wants to keep you from having is the Promise and Hope of Eternity with God.

*(Col. 1:27)* Just like there were giants on the path of the Israelites on their way to the Promised Land, today there are demonic beings doing everything possible to stop people from fulfilling their purpose and representing Jesus optimally in their spheres of influence. *(1Cor. 16:9)* These enemies' assignment is to populate hell with as many people as they can and depopulate Heaven.

The Battle of Eternal Security is a spiritual battle that involves keeping guard against these forces. There are demon spirits everywhere influencing humans to go against the Will of God. *(2Cor. 4:3-4)* Just as it was in the Garden of Eden when the devil deceived Eve and made Adam fall, so it is today.*(2Cor. 11:3)*

Apostle Paul in Ephesians 6 exhorts us in verse 13- *"having done all, to stand".* Paul is saying that once you have on the Armour, you have to keep it on, stand and use it and continue to use it to keep standing.

Here he implies we will be tempted to get into a relaxed mode. After winning the victory for which we may have prayed, fasted, and stood in faith, we tend to let our guards down, relax and then succumb to satan's assaults. Please understand that many times satan attacks after the victory due to our complacency. *(Amos 6:1)*

We must never get overconfident or complacent because 1Corinthians 10:12(NKJV) tells us, *"Let him who thinks he stands to take heed lest he falls."* The word “withstand” often implies successful resistance i.e., a resistance of two forces at opposite sides whereby the weakest link will give in.

(Remember that a chain is only as strong as its weakest link.) When you have done all according to the Word of God and it seems like nothing is happening, then stand.

This means you need to maintain the endurance to endure. Faith is a mustard seed yet has the tenacity and boldness of the righteous sustained by the Conquering Power of Christ. Stand firm, hold your ground and defend your territory against the enemy by submitting to God and hitting him hard in the Name of Jesus.

Many do not comprehend what Spiritual Warfare is all about. Because the Scripture says, *“For we wrestle not against flesh and blood, but against principalities, against powers, against rulers of darkness in this world and wicked spirits in the Heavenlies...."* (Eph. 6:12), they engage the devil as if in a practical wrestling contest. To correct this misconception, Van Raheenen wrote as follows: *"Spiritual warfare is not about fighting satan; he has been defeated by the Triumphal Resurrection of Jesus Christ. Spiritual warfare rather stands firm in Christ's Mighty Power.

It is accepting God's Victory through Christ by Faith and allowing God's Redemptive Power to work through Christ."* In other words, stand firm, resist the devil and enforce your victory. Your warfare has been accomplished and you have the victory. *(Isa. 40:2)* Prophet Amos said, *"Woe unto them that are at ease at Zion."* (Amos 6:1). We are soldiers and the enemy is watching and seeking an opportunity to strike

PRAYER:*

Father, we thank You for the Whole Armour You have given to us through the Sacrifice of

Jesus on the Cross of Calvary. We shall stand firm as good soldiers of Christ and die at our post while withstanding the evil days that are coming upon the Earth to the Glory of the Name of Jesus. Amen.

# Chapter 3

*Day 3: DAILY DEVOTIONAL*
*THE BENEFITS OF SERVICE*
*BIBLE READING: MATTHEW 20:27-28; JOHN 13:12-17; ACTS 9:1-6; MATTHEW 23:11-12*
*"Therefore, since we received a Kingdom which cannot be shaken, let us show gratitude, and offer to God pleasing service and acceptable worship with reverence and awe; for our, God is [indeed] a Consuming Fire." Hebrews 12:28-29 (AMP).*

The term service has diverse meanings depending on the context or usage which also affects the true meaning or attitude of a service provider.

The word “Service” simply means "the act of helping or working for someone which is either gratuitous or otherwise." It also means the giving of your resources, skills, time and the state of total surrender to a given task as evidenced by Apostle Paul after his Encounter with the Lord Jesus. *(Acts 9:1-6).* The Service in this context refers to Kingdom Service which is the advancement of the Affairs relating to the Kingdom of God and His Domain here on Earth.

Kingdom Service, therefore, is giving your all i.e., the totality of all you have, to the Work of God which is an expression of Love propelled by Revelation without compulsion. *(Heb. 6:12).*

Jesus Christ is the Greatest Servant in the Kingdom of God. *(Phil. 2:5-8).* He left His Throne above and made Himself of no reputation by taking the Form of a Servant to reconcile us back to the Father. *(2Cor. 5:18).* Jesus served to the extent that He washed His Own disciple's feet. *(Jn. 13:1-17).*

The reason God saved you is so you can serve. He said to Moses, *"Rise early in the morning and stand before Pharaoh; lo, he cometh forth to the water; and say unto him, "Thus saith the Lord, 'Let My people go that they may serve Me."* Ex. 8:20(KJV). Service is the pathway to honour in the Kingdom of God and we have highlighted some of its benefits:

*(1.) It guarantees God's Divine Presence:* When you are a committed Kingdom Servant, God's Presence will never leave you but shall be with you always. *(Josh. 1:9; Isa.43:2).*

*(2.) It guarantees God's Provision:* God is our Provider Who adds all things to us when

we seek and advance His Kingdom Agenda on Earth. *(Matt. 6:33; Ex.23:25).*

*(3.) It guarantees the Peace of God:* Peace is not the absence of turbulence but rest during the storm which God's Servants enjoy from the Prince of Peace Himself. *(Jn. 14:27; Ps. 85:8).*

*(4.) It guarantees Divine Promotion:* God is the Lifter of men. *(Ps. 75:6-7; Gen. 41:1-57).*

*(5.) It guarantees God's Protection:* God's faithful servants enjoy Divine Immunity and deliverance from evil projections. *(Dan. 3:27; Dan. 6:1-28).*

*(6.) It guarantees Eternal Security with God:* The Ultimate Benefit is the assurance of spending Eternity with God. *(Jn. 14:1-4; Dan.12:3)*

During a time like this, God looks for men, worthy vessels that He will use to accomplish His Great Purpose and make His Kingdom widely known.

The benefits of this Kingdom Service cannot be overemphasised because it is a fundamental condition for greatness. It is indeed a privilege for us to serve because if we fail to do so, stones would take our place. *(Lk. 19:39-40)* Don't be idle in our Father's House but rather join the Workforce of the Body of Christ and do the work while it is day because night shall come when no man can work. *(Jn. 9:4).*

*PRAYER:*
Heavenly Father, our lives are available to You. We will serve You with all our lives, wealth, skills, intellect, substance, time and everything in us. Give us the willingness to frequently hunger for your word and willingness to always hunger to be in your presence.

Knowing that our lives wholly depend on our service to you.
We will not withhold anything from You and shall give our all for the advancement of the Frontiers of Your Kingdom. In your vineyard, we shall always hunger to labour in Jesus' Mighty Name. Amen.

# Chapter 4

Day 4: DAILY DEVOTIONAL
THEIR WORKS DO FOLLOW THEM
BIBLE READING: MARK 10:29-30; 1CORINTHIANS 15:58; COLOSSIANS 4:12; 2CORINTHIANS 5:9-11; REVELATION 20:11-15

"Here is the patience of the saints; here are those who keep the Commandments of God and the Faith of Jesus. Then I heard a Voice from Heaven saying to me, "Write: 'Blessed are the dead who die in the Lord from now on." "Yes," says the Spirit, "that they may rest from their labours, and their works follow them."Revelation 14:12-13(NKJV)

The people of God who are called out from the world during this present age are described by the Apostle Paul as being a people "zealous of good works." (Tit. 2:14) Christianity for the followers of Jesus now means more than simply to be saved. The "Work" of the Church during this Age calls for all that the Christian possesses to perform it faithfully, hence the Christian life is portrayed in the Scriptures as one of sacrifice—a sacrifice which is completed only in death.

And it is only if we thus become dead with Him that we may hope to live with Him. It is this class, then—all of us who are following faithfully in the Footsteps of Jesus—who is now reckoned "dead" in God's Sight and who, in finishing our Earthly course, "die in the Lord." And "blessed" indeed are the particular "dead" ones referred to in our text.

For the assurance is that the completion of our sacrifice in actual death will not mean a cessation of our "work," because of us it is said, "their works do follow them." (Rev. 14:13) In other words, we will continue right on in the Work to which we were called.

Apostle Paul denotes this change by explaining that they will not sleep, while the Apostle John the Beloved indicates the same thing by saying that "their works do follow them." However, the great blessing of these is not that they are exempt from the necessity of dying because there is no exception to the Provision of the Divine Plan that only those who die in Christ will live with Him.

Yes, every follower of the Master must be "faithful unto death." (Rev. 2:10) But from a certain time onward—from "henceforth" those who die in the Lord will not need to remain asleep in death. Paul explains the matter, saying that there shall be "changed, in a moment, in the twinkling of an eye." (1Cor. 15:51-52).

Whether good or bad, the influence of our lives continues to impact others even after we are gone. This is a sobering reality. It is a source of joy if we have laboured for the Lord in this life. It is a source of grief if we have laboured for ourselves. The souls that we win and disciple to Jesus will extend the fruit of our labour into many generations to come.

One day we will all appear before the Judgment Seat of Christ where we will be judged according to our works. *(2Cor. 5:10)* Those who have died in the Lord are currently at rest from their labours as they await the Judgment Seat of Christ.

Why is it that these saints who have died must wait until the End to receive their rewards? It is because their lives are still bearing fruit. Although they are at rest from their "labours," their "Works" continue to follow them. Therefore, they cannot be judged until their "Works" are finished.

In summary, our lives will not be evaluated by what we have accomplished in our lifetime alone. We will also be judged by the impact of our lives upon future generations. Therefore, we should judge nothing before the time when Christ Himself will evaluate the final fruit of our labours. We should be diligent in this life to labour for what will survive us. Those who do will be blessed. They will one day rest from their labours and rejoice because their Works continue to follow them.

These works are laborious now. They cost suffering, misunderstanding, sacrifice and toil. But despite the cost, it is our privilege to continue “abounding in the Work of the Lord.” (1Cor. 15:58) Today we “stand in jeopardy,” we may have “afflictions,” “necessities,” and “distresses.” (1Cor. 15:30; 2Cor. 6:4-5)

There may indeed come “imprisonments,” “tumults,” and “labours,” but let us continue faithfully in the Lord’s Work. Let us be faithful even unto death, comforted with the Precious Promise that if now we thus “die in the Lord,” there will come “rest from our labours,” but the Glorious Work of the Lord, the Work of reconciling the lost world to Himself (2Cor. 5:18-20) would be continued in Glory, without labour and suffering.

PRAYER:
Heavenly Father, we ask You to forgive us for limiting Your Work to our generation. O Lord, please grant us a Revelation of the impact that our lives can have upon generations after us. Give us Your Vision to lay foundations in our lifetime that other

generations can build upon. Help us to sow seeds that will continue to bear fruit long after we are gone. So that even when we are departed from this world, our good works will continue to speak for us. Your gospel will continue to move from one generation to another till the end of time. As we do this, may your blessings remain with us in Jesus's Mighty Name. Amen.

# Chapter 5

*Day 5: DAILY DEVOTIONAL*
*THE BAPTISM OF HIS SUFFERINGS*
*BIBLE READING: MATTHEW 4:1; MARK 10:29-31; ACTS 14:22; JAMES 1:2-4*

" *But Jesus answered and said, “You do not know what you ask. Are you able to drink the Cup that I am about to drink, and be baptized with the Baptism that I am baptized with?" They said to Him, "We are able." Matthew 20:22 (NKJV* )

Suffering is an inevitable part of the Salvation Package and the Christian Maturity Process which every believer is expected to partake of. The Bible makes it abundantly clear that suffering for the sake of the Kingdom was a great privilege indeed: "And they departed from the presence of the council, rejoicing that they were counted worthy to suffer shame for His Name." Acts 5:41(KJV)

The quality of our Faith in Him isn't known until it is tested hence suffering for the Sake of Jesus and His Kingdom was a thing of great joy. (Jam. 1:2) Until you've been tested, you can never become a testimony.

There is a difference between the SUBSTITUTION of Christ in suffering and the EXAMPLE of Christ in suffering. Apostle Peter clarified this by stating: " *For this you were called, because Christ also suffered for us, leaving us an example, that you should follow His Steps." 1Pet. 2:21(NKJV)* Jesus Christ took our place as our Substitute, suffering during His Passion Week so that we wouldn't have to. On the flip side, He also suffered persecution, revilement and slander, serving as our Example of how to act whenever we find ourselves in a similar situation. (1Pet. 2:22-23)

An understanding of "the Fellowship of His Sufferings..." (Phil. 3:10c) helps us trace what Dr Kenneth E. Hagin of blessed memory would call "The Way of the Spirit" (Ecc. 11:5a) i.e., the DNA of God amid our daily circumstances. There are Four Categories of Suffering we are expected to pass through as Christian believers to become mature:

(1.) Trials: These are those tests which are initiated directly by the Lord God Almighty Himself. (1Pet. 5:10) God never uses sickness or infirmities to afflict His children hence the English Term "afflictions" is translated from the Greek Word "thlipsis" which means "tests or trials."

(2.) Temptations: These are those tests which are directly initiated by Satan himself. (Jam. 1:13-15) The devil tempts Christian believers in a bid to undermine our Faith and produce sin consciousness within, diminishing their confidence in the Lord. (Lk. 22:31-32)

(3.) Persecutions: These are those tests that are directly initiated by individuals or people who hinder the Move of God in the life of the Christian believer, knowingly or unknowingly. (Matt. 5:11-12) Persecution comes with the territory hence every Christian must be willing to embrace it. (2Tim. 3:12)

(4.) Tribulations: These are those tests which are directly initiated by environmental factors such as hostile administrations. (Jn. 16:33) The Lord Jesus is still in the Business of building up His Church on the Rock and the gates of hell can never prevail. ( *Matt. 16:18* ) We remain confident that whatever form of Suffering always turns out for our good, regardless of the devil's plans. ( *Gen. 50:20* ) To Him alone be all the Glory!

*PRAYER* :
Heavenly Father, we honour You for deeming us worthy to suffer for Your Sake and the Gospel. O Lord, please grant us the Wisdom to distinguish each category of suffering and to see Your Hand behind the scenes in Jesus' Mighty Name. Amen.

# Chapter 6

Day 6: DAILY DEVOTIONAL

OBTAINING THE CROWN OF RIGHTEOUSNESS

BIBLE READING: DANIEL 12:13; ACTS 13:36; 2TIMOTHY 4:6-8

"And say to Archippus, "Take heed to the ministry which you have received in the Lord, that you may fulfill it." Colossians 4:17(NKJV)

There is no greater privilege on Earth than being enrolled in the Service of the Lord God Almighty Himself. One of the most influential and powerful offices under the Sun is that of the POTUS (President Of The United States). However, the American Constitution allows for no more than two terms for anyone seeking that lofty position. This means that the American president is limited in the scope and duration of his power which is a maximum of eight years or two four-year terms in office.

By contrast, the Scriptures state that those Christian believers who are part of the First Resurrection would reign with the Lord Jesus for a thousand years during the Millennium. (Rev. 20:6) This amounts to two hundred and fifty (250) consecutive terms in power AS A MERE FORETASTE of our Eternal Reign with Him! Food for thought indeed but the reality is that a crown as we examined in our previous devotional, is proof that one is qualified to rule with the Lord. One of the most important of them all is the Crown of Righteousness.

The Bible refers to the Crown of Righteousness as a reward from the Lord Jesus Christ to Christian believers who faithfully fulfil God's Divine Assignment or Purpose for their lives. Apostle John the Beloved said that "For THIS PURPOSE the Son of God was manifested, that He might destroy the works of the devil." (1Jn. 3:8b) Apostle Paul was mindful of his imminent martyrdom via beheading at the hands of Emperor Nero which informed his second epistle to his spiritual son Timothy.

He emphasized his readiness to be reunited with the Lord Jesus Christ which then begs the question: What gave him the effrontery to claim the Crown of Righteousness? The threefold answer is seen in 2Timothy 4:7:
(1.) I have fought a good fight... Firstly, the only good fight every Christian believer must engage in is the Good Fight of Faith. (1Tim. 6:12) We must never forget that the righteous live and are sustained by Faith alone. (Hab. 2:4)
(2.) I have finished MY course... Secondly, Paul stated he had finished HIS course i.e., his God-given Ministry or Assignment. God will never commend you for doing what He never commanded you to do in the first place.
(3.) I have kept THE Faith... Finally, Paul kept or guarded the Christian Faith. We must always contend for the Faith because

whatever we're called to do must be a witness or testimony in the eyes of all to our New Life in Christ. (Jude 3) Pursuing God's Agenda without portraying His Moral Attributes is counterproductive.

The primary goal of every disciple of Jesus Christ ought to be Christlikeness which is the end of all spiritual warfare. The Scriptures state clearly: "So I run straight towards the goal to win the prize, which is God's Call through Christ Jesus to the Life above." Phil. 3:14(GNT) This goal is what qualifies us and enables us to fulfil God's Divine Call upon our lives. Let us strive to become more like Him and finish the ministry He gave us, ther

PRAYER:
Heaven father, Grant us the Grace to accomplish your work to qualify for the Crown of Righteousness in Jesus' Mighty Name. Amen.

# Chapter 7

Day 7: DAILY DEVOTIONAL

RECEIVING STRENGTH ON THE MOUNTAIN OF FAMILY

BIBLE READING: GENESIS 18:18-19; PSALM 68:6; LUKE 2:52; PSALM 22:27

"Behold, I will send you Elijah the prophet before the Coming of the Great and Dreadful Day of the Lord. And he will turn the hearts of the fathers to the children, and the hearts of the children to their fathers, lest I come and strike the Earth with a curse." Malachi 4:5-6(NKJV)

One of the major characteristics of the Enoch/Elijah Revolution which is fast approaching in these End Times is the Restoration of the Father-Son Order, which is at the core of the family unit.

The family unit is the foundation of the society while the foundation of the family unit is the Authentic Man whom the

Scripture affirms to be "complete in Him Who is the Head of all principality and powers." (Col. 2:10)

A strong society is the direct result of strong families which are in turn made up of strong individuals.

When the Lord God Almighty gave Adam the Dominion Mandate, He gave him the blueprint for establishing authentic families that mirror the Order of Heaven. (Gen. 1:26-28)

All dysfunctional individuals such as corrupt government officials, ritualists and street urchins are products of dysfunctional families.

The onus, therefore, lies upon us as genuine Christian parents to regulate the moral tide of society by raising Godly children according to the Biblical Template, (Prov. 22:6) thereby blessing our communities with assets rather than liabilities. It is commonly said that "Charity begins at home." This is true because the Family Institution was designed by God to be the parent institution to the Church, the schools and the government. Let us never forget that our children in life would be remembered for either of two things: The problems they helped solve which is our utmost desire or the problems they helped create. The Lord continue granting us Mercy and Grace for the task ahead.

PRAYER:

Heavenly Father, we ascribe all the Glory to You alone. O Lord, please help us to effectively raise Godly seed who will possess the gates of Your enemies. May our children not be like the sons of Eli, may our children not be vagabonds but Godly men and women who will carry on the gospel in Jesus' Mighty Name. Amen.

# Chapter 8

## Day 8: DAILY DEVOTIONAL
## THE SHEPHERD'S CROWN

BIBLE READING: PROVERBS 27:23-27; JOHN 10:11-17; 1PETER 5:1-4

"Therefore take heed to yourselves and to all the flock, among which the Holy Spirit has made you overseers, to shepherd the Church of God which He purchased with His Blood." Acts 20:28(NKJV)

The Lord Jesus Christ has raised us as Christian believers to be kings and priests, sharing in the administration of God's Universe which even transcends time. (2Tim. 2:12) Throughout the Scriptures, we can see that a crown is ample evidence of one's qualification to reign with Christ Jesus. One such is called Shepherd's Crown or the Crown of Glory.

The Shepherd's Crown is the reward of Jesus to those who have been found faithful in the matter of Spiritual Oversight. What this means is that this is the Lord's reward to those believers who faithfully execute the office of a spiritual elder or pastor specifically as well as those who faithfully look after a group or groups of believers placed under their care.

People who qualify are those who manifest the Attributes of Jesus Christ, the Good Shepherd Himself Who feeds and cares for His sheep. (Jn. 21:15-17) This requires having a pastoral heart.

The way someone may prophesy without being a prophet or win souls without being an evangelist is the same way one can groom and care for others spiritually without being called a pastor.

Simply put, any disciple of Jesus Christ can qualify for the Shepherd's Crown provided he's willing to pay the price.

King David was established as king over Israel, wielding tremendous power and influence yet was willing to lay down his life and the lives of his family members to avert a plague which was the result of his unauthorized census of Israel.

As the shepherd, he appealed to God on behalf of his subjects and asked "But these sheep, what have they done?" (2Sam. 24:17) Only a genuine pastor would think that way.

The Bible admonishes us to diligently know the state of our flocks and attend to our herds for "RICHES are not forever nor does A CROWN endure to all generations." (Prov. 27:24) From the aforementioned verse, we can notice two major wrong motives for entering the pastoral office:

(1.) Riches or Wealth: We must provide Spiritual Oversight for the outcome rather than the income. (1Pet. 5:2)

(2.) A Crown or Popularity: When we lift Jesus in the lives of our people, He will draw all men, faithful pastors inclusive, unto Himself. (Jn. 12:32) We must avoid getting into ministry for the sake of accolades or fame and exalt the Lord Jesus in the lives of those we oversee that He may exalt us in their sight. May we receive at His Appearing a Crown of Glory "that does not fade away." (1Pet. 5:4)

PRAYER:
Heavenly Father, thank You for being our Chief Shepherd. O Lord, we humbly ask that You instil within us a pastoral heart so that we may genuinely care for Your sheepLord, in Jesus' Mighty Name. Amen

# Chapter 9

Day 9: DAILY DEVOTIONAL

BEING BOLD ON THE DAY OF JUDGMENT

BIBLE READING: ROMANS 14:10; REVELATION 20:11-15; 1JOHN 4:17-18; REVELATIONl 22:10-15

For we must all appear before the Judgment Seat of Christ, that each one may receive the things done in the body, according to what he has done, whether good or bad." 2Corinthians 5:10(NKJV)

Whenever the subject of judgment is brought up by most Christian believers, there is usually an air of apprehension and terror. Divine Judgment is one of the least anticipated encounters of most genuine believers in the Full Gospel of our Lord Jesus Christ. However, the subject of God's Judgment is inevitable according to the Holy Scriptures: "And as it is appointed for men to die once, but after this the Judgment." Heb. 9:27 (NKJV)

There are Two Major Types of Divine Judgment to look forward to on the Last Day:

(1.) The Great White Throne: This is the judgment of those unbelievers whose names are omitted from the Book of Life. (Rev. 20:11-15) God the Father would preside over this judgment which would spell Eternal Damnation for those who have never accepted the Lord Jesus as Saviour and Lord.

(2.) The Judgment Seat of Christ: This is the judgment of Christian believers which would be presided over by the Lord Jesus Christ Himself. (Rom. 14:10) The primary focus of this form of judgment is rewarding for faithfulness in Christian Service. The Greek Word translated "Judgment Seat" here is "Bema" which refers to "a rostrum or podium upon which judges tower above those about to be judged. Simply put, the Lord Jesus came to save us as the Lamb of God but would judge us as the Lion of the Tribe of Judah.

Having the boldness as Christian believers to face the Lord on the Day of Judgment and anticipate His Words of Commendation "Well done, good and faithful servant..." (Matt. 25:21a) is only probable if our Love for Him and others is perfect. The word "perfect" here is translated from the Greek Word "teleios" which means "mature". (1Jn. 4:17-18) May the Lord open our eyes to this Reality.

PRAYER

Heavenly Father, we thank You for delivering us from the Great White Throne Judgment. O Lord, please sustain us by Your Mercy and Grace as we look forward to the Judgment Seat of Christ in Jesus' Mighty Name. Amen.

# Chapter 10

*Day 10: DAILY DEVOTIONAL*
*COMMUNICATION IN MARRIAGE*
BIBLE READING: COLOSSIANS 4:6; PROVERBS 31:26; PROVERBS 12:18.*

*“She openeth her mouth with Wisdom, and in her tongue is the Law of Kindness." Proverbs 31:26(KJV)*

The lifeblood of every relationship is communication. In other words, what blood is to the human body is what communication is to every relationship, marriage inclusive. *(1Pet. 3:7)*

It runs through every aspect of marriage because once there is a communication breakdown, it affects many things and opens the door for the enemy. This is one major reason an understanding of the purpose and power of communication is critical in relationships at large.

Communication is the ability to transmit thoughts and perceptions between two people. In male and female differences, women communicate emotionally (based on how they feel) while men communicate logically (based on thinking, facts and reasoning). It is noteworthy that we interpret things based on how we perceive them because perception is stronger than reality. *(Ex. 32:17-18)*

There are Three Key Elements in Effective Communication:
*(1.) The Actual Content:* This refers to the real words spoken audibly which makes up only 7% of Communication. *(Eph. 4:29)*

*(2.) The Tone of the Voice:* This conditions the perception of the person with

whom we communicate and makes up 38% of the Communication. *(Prov. 15:1)*

*(3.) Non-verbal Communication:* This refers to signs, gestures, facial expressions, body language etc. These make up 55% of Effective Communication. It is advisable in communication not to talk when one is angry because you won't communicate well and may say things that you would regret afterwards. In correction, learn to always sandwich commendation with correction in between so your spouse won't be a victim of destructive criticism. Learn to overlook certain things while also sitting down to discuss certain sensitive issues.

The following are Obstacles to Communication:
*(a.) Lack of Truthfulness:* It creates suspicion and distrust so be open-minded, as well as transparent with your spouse.

*(b.) Lack of Exclusivity:* Love is jealous just like the Lord God Almighty Himself.*(Exo 20: 5)*
As married couples, we must set boundaries with the opposite sex because there is a place in our hearts that only our spouses should occupy. Love needs to be serviced by communication.

*(c.) Defensiveness:* When your spouse is telling you something about you, listen and don't be defensive.

*(d.) Failure to listen:* Spend quality time together and practice active listening as you express your thoughts, feelings and aspirations to each other. When there is a communication breakdown, satan starts

*PRAYER:*
Lord, please grant us the Grace and Wisdom to communicate effectively with our spouses in Jesus' Mighty Name. Amen.

# Chapter 11

Day 11: DAILY DEVOTIONAL
REIGNING WITH HIM IN ETERNITY
BIBLE READING: ISAIAH 2:1-3; MICAH 4:1-2; REVELATION 5:1-12; REVELATION 11:15

"Favoured and Holy are those who have a share in the First Resurrection. The second death has no power over them, but they will be the priests of God and Christ, and will rule with Him for one thousand years." Revelation 20:6(Common English Bible)

A Total Redemption was the Primary Motive that prompted the Sacrifice of our Lord Jesus Christ upon the Cross. When He said "It is finished.." (Jn. 19:30), He was referring to the Truth that the Price for the Redemption of man and his environment had been paid in full i.e., from the Greek Word "Tetelestai." He did this so that indeed He might be known as the Lord of all. (Phil. 2:9-11)

When Jesus was tempted by the devil in the wilderness, the latter made Him an offer regarding the kingdoms of this world: "Then the devil, taking Him up on a high mountain, showed Him all the kingdoms of the world in a moment." (Lk. 4:5)

The Greek term translated into the English word "kingdoms" is "basileia", which means "realm or rule." This means that Satan showed the Lord Jesus something other than literal kingdoms with geographic boundaries, quite contrary to orthodox belief.

The tempter offered Jesus the Seven Mountains of Society or the Seven Major

Realms of Influence (Rev. 5:12) on the condition that He would worship him. However, the Lord would never even think of compromising the Divine Process involved in redeeming the aforementioned kingdoms. (Ps. 110:1) The only way His enemies can become His Footstool is when He receives the following from the Church, thereby empowering us to reign forever with Him:

(1.) Power: Jesus will receive this on the Mountain of Government. (Isa. 9:6-7)

(2.) Riches: Jesus will receive this on the Mountain of Economy. (Phil. 4:19)

(3.) Wisdom: Jesus will receive this on the Mountain of Education. (Isa. 54:13)

(4.) Strength: Jesus will receive this on the Mountain of Family. (Mal. 4:5-6)

(5.) Honour: Jesus will receive this on the Mountain of Worship/Religion. (Jn. 4:23-24)

(6.) Glory: Jesus will receive this on the Mountain of Celebration of Arts and Entertainment. (Ps. 16:11)
(7.) Blessing: Jesus will receive this on the Mountain of Communication/Media. (Isa. 52:7)

This is the Grand Master Plan of the Lord God Almighty. The kingdoms of this world would truly become the kingdoms of our Lord and His Christ in reality after Christians arise as revivalists and reformers. (Rev. 11:15) God is counting on us to bring the Total Influence of Christianity and the Kingdom of God upon these Seven Mountains of Society.

PRAYER:
Heavenly Father, we thank You for the Power of Your Total Redemption. O Lord, please help us take our place as the Body of Christ as we leverage on the gains of the End Time Revival by possessing the Seven

Realms of Society for the Sake of the Kingdom in Jesus' Mighty Name. Amen.

# Chapter 12

Day 12: DAILY DEVOTIONAL
HOW TO CHOOSE RIGHT
BIBLE READING: PROVERBS 24: 3-6; GENESIS 2:18; PROVERBS 15:21

"Every purpose is established by counsel: and with good advice make war." Proverbs 20:18(KJV).

The greatest discovery anyone can make, with the sole exception of a decision for Christ and a discovery of purpose, is the choice of a spouse. The Bible tells us that "none shall want her mate..."(Isa. 34:16b) which means everybody has someone assigned by the Lord God Almighty as the right spouse who will complement his or her Divine Calling.

Apart from spiritual homogeneity, there are some basic principles to put into consideration before we decide who to get married to. These principles are seeking counsel, having a Unity of Purpose and having complementary personalities:

(1.) SEEK COUNSEL: Proverbs 24:3-4(TLB) says, "Any house is built by wise planning, becomes strong through common sense, and profits wonderfully by keeping abreast of the facts." After you have heard from God, you need Godly Counsel. We can liken marriage to an enterprise that we intend to build hence the admonition to seek much counsel. Prov. 15:21(NIV). Many marriages are experiencing avoidable heartache today because they refused to seek counsel. (Ps. 1:1 KJV). You can either run your relationship by Hollywood or by the Holy Word. It was Jonadab's advice to Ammon the son of David in 2Samuel 13 that made him commit incest which resulted in his death.

2. UNITY OF PURPOSE: Marriage is an alignment of purposes. Someone defined marriage as *"the coming together of a man and a woman from two different nations to create a new nation whose culture will promote the best interest of every citizen and give the world rest."* In a marriage, both parties come into the relationship with their purposes and visions which have to be harnessed for the common good of the family. Purpose and vision are resources to be aligned together. Marriage ought not to be a disruptor of the visions of both parties.

3. COMPLEMENTARY PERSONALITIES: Our personalities play a large role in the success or failure of our relationships. Taking personality tests is encouraged for would-be couples and those already in marriage. You need a good knowledge of yourself in other to make the necessary adjustments that are required in marriage.

Your personality has to complement that of your intended life partner.

Your temperament is not something you wish away, rather it is your make-up that you need to understand and improve on by renewing your mind with the Word of God to enable you to enhance your relationship. (Rom. 12:2) You should know and understand your personality type, which will give you an insight into your strengths and weaknesses.

You should also assess the personality of your chosen life partner, to better understand them and to know their strengths and weaknesses as well. This will help you to complement each other so that you emphasize your strengths and help each other balance out your weaknesses.

PRAYER:
Heavenly Father, we thank You for granting us the power to choose right. O Lord, please

enlighten the eyes of our hearts as we choose the right spouses for our prophetic destinies in Jesus' Mighty Name. Amen.

# Chapter 13

Day 13: DAILY DEVOTIONAL
PARENTING ACCORDING TO THE SCRIPTURES
BIBLE READING: GENESIS 1:28; TITUS 2:4-5; PSALM 127:3-5; PROVERBS 22:6; GENESIS 18:18-19

"For I know him, that he will command his children and his household after him, and they shall keep the Way of the Lord, to do Justice and Judgment, that the Lord may bring upon Abraham that which He hath spoken of him." Genesis 18:19(KJV)

Parenting is the act of raising children following Set Biblical Rules for an expected end. (Prov. 22:6) Parenting is a Command from the Lord. From the above Scripture, we are expected to train our children in the way they should go.

This shows that parenting is a responsibility and that only responsible parenting according to the Scriptures yields good results. There are different ways of parenting, but we shall be considering parenting according to the Scriptural Guidelines. The foundation of proper parenting is the Christian marriage i.e., a man and woman living together under the ordinance of marriage. (Mal. 2:15)

Responsible parenting starts with a good marriage, hence we should give adequate attention to our relationships with our spouses and mend any foundational cracks because "If the foundations are destroyed, what can the righteous do?" (Ps. 11:3)

If you are not yet married but desire to raise godly children, lay a good foundation by following Biblical Principles of choosing a life partner.

For those already married, revisit your foundation by maintaining a good attitude towards your spouse. Your attitude towards your spouse determines your children's attitudes toward both of you. When you respect one another, the children naturally respect you and your laws. Do not fight with your spouse, especially in front of your child(ren). It is not too late for anyone to begin responsible parenting. The Spirit of God will perfect it if you allow Him. A healthy marriage makes for good parenting.

Your children must see you and your spouse as one because you are in this business of parenting together, therefore, you must join forces to make it a success. (Amos 3:3)

The following are some Basic Guidelines for proper parenting in God's Programme:
(1.) It is a Command from the Lord. Prov. 22:6; Psalm 127:3-5; Gen. 18:18-19

(2.) God expects diligence and a sense of responsibility in your parenting: (Psalm 127:4)

(3.) Parenting should be done together by the man and the woman: (Prov. 1:8)
(4.) The gross responsibility lies on the man: (Prov. 4:1-4; Gen. 18:19; 1Tim. 3:4) Every married man must manage his household without losing his dignity.

There are certain ways to lead your children in a life of Godliness in Christ:
(a.) Dedicate your children to God at the beginning of their lives (even before and after conception): 1Sam. 1:28; Lk. 2:22.

(b.) Teach your children to fear the Lord and turn away from evil, to love righteousness and to hate iniquity: Instill in them an awareness of God's Attitude and Judgment towards sin. (Heb 1:9)

(c.) Teach them to obey you as parents through Biblical Discipline: Deut. 8:5; Prov. 3:11-12; 13:24; 23:13-14; 29:15,17; Heb. 12:7.

(d.) Protect your children from ungodly influences by being aware of Satan's attempts to destroy them spiritually through attraction to the world or through immoral companions: Prov. 13:20; 28:7; 1Jn. 2:15-17.

(e.) Make them aware that God is always observing and evaluating what they do, think and say: Ps. 139:1-12.

(f.) Bring them early in life to personal Faith, Repentance and Water Baptism in Christ: Matt. 19:14.

PRAYER:

Heavenly Father, we thank You for the privilege of parenthood. Please grant us the Grace to be responsible parents to train our children in Your Ways in Jesus' Mighty Name. Amen.

# Chapter 14

*Day 14: DAILY DEVOTIONAL*
THE FAMILY THAT PRAYS TOGETHER STAYS TOGETHER*

*BIBLE READING: PSALM 133:1-3; EPHESIANS 3:17-20; ACTS 2:42-47; 1PETER 3:7*
*"Even them I will bring to My Holy Mountain, and make them joyful in My House of Prayer. Their burnt offerings and their sacrifices will be accepted on My Altar, for My House shall be called a House of Prayer for all nations." Isaiah 56:7(NKJV)*

Prayer is a very powerful tool which unites people together in Love. There's this general saying that "a family that prays together stays together." This is so true because genuine prayer is a critical aspect of koinonia *(2Cor. 13:14)* which must be present in every healthy relationship.

The bonding capabilities of effective prayer can never be overemphasized.

Prayer can generate intimacy. In other words, we fall in love with three categories of people: The Person to Whom we pray, with whom we pray and for whom we pray.

*(1.) The Person to Whom we pray:* When we spend quality time praying to God in fellowship, we get deeper and intimate with Him and our spirits are united with the Spirit of God. We become one literally with Him, His Purpose, Will and Mind. *(1Cor. 6:17)*

*(2.) The people with whom we pray:* When we spend time with one another in a cooperative setting e.g., family, prayer partner, Church, etc., it enables us to maintain the Unity of the Spirit in the Bond of Peace. *(Eph. 4:3).*

*(3.) The person for whom we pray:* The Scripture admonishes us to pray for certain people e.g., those in Authority, *(1Tim. 2:1-2)* one another *(Jam. 5:16)* and for your enemies. *(Matt. 5:44)* Praying together was one of the secrets of Unity and Strength of the Early Church. *(Acts 2:42-47).*

Love is what unites people because we fall deeper in Love with other brethren when we constantly fellowship with one another in all sincerity and truth. The same principle applies in our domestic families hence it is of the utmost importance that every serious family must establish a strong and potent family altar which would only cause all to wax stronger.

*PRAYER:*
O God, we ask You for Grace to always discipline ourselves to fellowship with one another in Jesus' Mighty Name.

# Chapter 15

Day 15: DAILY DEVOTIONAL
ARE YOU A FRIEND OR ARE YOU BEING FRIENDLY?

BIBLE READING: PSALM 41:9; JOB 2:11; PSALM 55:12-14; ZECHARIAH 13:6-7
"You are My friends if you do whatever I command you. No longer do I call you servants, for a servant does not know what his master is doing, but I have called you

friends, for all things that I heard from My Father I have made known to you." John 15:14-15(NKJV)

There is a difference between being friends with some and at the same time being friendly with others. The former focuses on the building of alliances and fellowships (Prov. 18:24b) while the latter refers to congeniality i.e., the skill involved in socializing and getting along with the vast majority of people.

The Scriptures tell us that "A friend loves at all times, and a brother is born for adversity." (Prov. 17:17) Simply put, genuine friends stay committed to their friends even through thick and thin.

Friendship is one of the most abused and misunderstood concepts in the social sphere. The sad reality is that very few know the line between mere acquaintances and actual friends. Diplomacy and common ground are required when it comes to being friendly while compatibility of purpose and vision must be involved when making genuine friends. (Lk. 1:39-56) Genuine friendship creates intimacy but intimacy creates vulnerability.

PRAYER:
Heavenly Father, to You alone, do we ascribe all the Glory. O Lord, please assist us in locating those friends that would boost our destinies in Jesus' Mighty Name. Amen.

# Chapter 16

Day 16: DAILY DEVOTIONAL
THE IMPORTANCE OF FAITHFULNESS IN RELATIONSHIPS

BIBLE READING: PROVERBS 20:6; 1THESSALONIANS 5:24; PROVERBS 28:20; PROVERBS 3:3-4

"Let love and faithfulness never leave you; bind them around your neck, write them on the tablet of your heart. Then you will win favour and a good name in the sight of God and man." Proverbs 3:3-4(NIV)

Faithfulness can be defined as loyalty or the ability to be trusted. Faithfulness is the cornerstone of the character of a person and a mandatory requirement for all Christians: "Moreover it is required in stewardship that a man be found faithful." (1Cor. 4:2)

Everyone irrespective of gender or class requires their colleagues, spouse, friends etc., to be faithful to them in thoughts and deeds. Faithfulness is becoming increasingly scarce in human relationships because people often breach the terms of engagement or engage in anti-covenant practices hence the continuous search for faithful men: "Most men will proclaim each his goodness, but who can find a faithful man?" (Prov. 20:6).

Faithfulness is a fundamental virtue required from every man by God, which is why it is one of the Fruits of the Spirit: "But the Fruit of the Spirit is Love, Joy, Peace, Longsuffering, Goodness, Kindness, Faithfulness, Gentleness, Self-control against such there is no law." Gal. 5:22-23(NKJV).

As a Christian, it is important to exhibit these Fruits of the Spirit in our lives and relationships with others. A faithful individual is given assurance or one who is bound by a promise to always deliver. God was so Faithful in His Relationship with the man that He sent His Only Son to die on the Cross so that our sins would be forgiven and we would obtain Eternal Life. (Jn. 3:16) The Price Jesus paid was a Sacrifice of His Own Life and it is a cost you must be prepared to pay in your relationships.

The Bible is clear that faithfulness requires sacrifice. In no verse is this stated more poignantly than in John 15:13(NKJV) where we read: "Greater love has no one than this than to lay down one's life for his friends." There is no better example of loving one's neighbour as yourself than being willing to die for them, just as Christ died for you and me.

The importance of faithfulness in relationships with God or between men cannot be overemphasized. Being faithful encourages your spouse, partner or colleague to be faithful to you. It increases the longevity of your relationship, gives you peace of mind, makes you focus on your relationship/marriage to have a healthy relationship, keeps you and your family safe etc. Unfaithfulness is a vice that should not be justified or entertained because it ruins trust and destroys good relationships. (Prov. 25:19)

PRAYER:
Father, we thank You for the gift of relationships and the people You have placed in our lives. We desire to be faithful in our dealings with others and on the assignments that You and the authority figures that we are answerable to have committed to our trust. May we receive the Grace to be faithful and honest in our relationship with everyone around us. Father, please help us to impact everything that is around us positively for Your Glory in Jesus' Name. Amen.

# Chapter 17

*Day 17: DAILY DEVOTIONAL*
*ISOLATION BEFORE DESTRUCTION*

*BIBLE READING: EXODUS 18:13-26; PROVERBS 18:1; ECCLESIASTES 4:9-10; JOHN 10:1-30*

The Scriptures make it clear to us that the Lord is our Shepherd and His Ultimate Desire is to have one flock under One Shepherd. *(Ps. 23:1; Jn.10:16)* From this we must understand that the security of every sheep is found in two major factors i.e., the shepherd and the sheepfold. *(Lk. 15:3-7)* Given this, the devil's strategy has remained constant over the years: *(1.) Isolate Christian believers from the fortress of both the Shepherd and the sheepfold:* This is accomplished through factors such as ignorance, offence and rebellion.
*(2.) Destroy the gullible ones who have fallen into his age-old trap.*

Moses the lawgiver was completely overwhelmed by the daily demands of close to three million Israelites and cried out in frustration to the Lord: *"I am not able to bear all these people alone, because the burden is too heavy for me. If You treat me like this, please kill me here and now—if I have found favour in Your Sight—and do not let me see my wretchedness."* (Num. 11:14-15)

There is only so much that can be achieved by one person in isolation hence the need for synergy. One of the surest routes to stagnation and burnout is "the lone ranger syndrome." The man was designed by the Lord God Almighty to interact and relate with others hence the one who is rich in relationships is rich indeed.

*PRAYER:*

Heavenly Father, please grant us the Grace and discipline to remain planted amongst the saints and not stray away from Your Presence in Jesus' Mighty Name. Amen.

# Chapter 18

*Day 18: DAILY DEVOTIONAL*
*THE POWER OF AGREEMENT*

*GENESIS 11:6; AMOS 3:3; ECCLESIASTES 4:9-12; 1PETER 3:7*
"Again I say unto you, that if two of you shall agree on Earth as touching anything that they shall ask, it shall be done for them of My Father which is in Heaven. For where two or three are gathered together in My Name, there am I in the midst of them." Matthew 18:19-20(KJV)*

There is a difference between Unity and Conformity. To have Unity, there is a need for an Agreement regarding the very important aspects of that union or relationships like the vision, the language and the mission that will hold the people together. *(Gen. 1:26)* Conformity involves people agreeing on the surface while being opposed to each other as regards the very important things concerning them.

Marriage provides the best platform for people to explore the Power of Unity. This Power is explored through sharing a common vision and language *(Gen. 11:6)* through prayer and through engaging in a common activity. *(Amos 3:3).* It is so critical that the Bible warns men against maltreating their wives because one of the consequences is that their prayers would be hindered if they do so. *(1 Pet. 3:7).*

Nothing will be impossible to accomplish when people are united in agreement with each other. The only way to defeat such people is to bring disunity among them. That is why God in Genesis 11 to defeat a united people had to confuse their language. When people are speaking a different language they cannot understand themselves or agree with each other.

And that is why the devil always seeks to bring disunity, disagreement and division in marriages and other organizations that are a threat to him.

We must use every opportunity and ability we have to fight for Unity and Agreement in our Marriages, Churches, Organizations and among the different people groups in our nation. The Scriptures admonish us to endeavour to keep the Unity of the Spirit in the Bond of Peace. *(Eph. 4:3).* There is no obstacle we cannot overcome as long as we are united in agreement with one another. The Power of Agreement is what makes the Trinity or the Godhead *(God the Father, God the Son and God the Holy Spirit)* the Most Powerful Union in existence.

PRAYER:*

Lord, please grant us an understanding of the Power of Agreement and Unity and help us to strive towards it in our Marriages, Churches, Organizations and Nation in Jesus' Mighty Name. Amen

# Chapter 19

## Day 19: DAILY DEVOTIONAL
## THE BIBLICAL VIEW ON PREMARITAL SEX

BIBLE READING: 1THESSALONIANS 4:3-4; EXODUS 22:16; HEBREWS 13:4
"Now as to the matters of which you wrote: It is good (beneficial, advantageous) for a man not to touch a woman [outside marriage]. But because of [the temptation to participate in] sexual immorality, let each man have his wife, and let each woman have her husband." 1Corinthians 7:1-2(Amplified Bible)

One of the most rapidly increasing grey areas within the Christian Context is the issue of sexual intimacy. As a result of the slow but steady permeation of false doctrines which promote lawlessness within the Church, several have abandoned Basic Biblical Boundaries for the sake of inclusion. (2Tim. 4:3-4)

Sex could be defined as a process of intimate intercourse between a man and a woman within the Context of the Biblical Marriage Covenant. (Gen. 2:24) There are three major purposes of sexual intercourse i.e., covenant bonding, procreation and sensual pleasure based on Scriptural Standards. Premarital sex is a no-no because sex was designed by God to be enjoyed only within the marital union. The Bible states emphatically:
"But sexual sin is never right: Our bodies were not made for that but the Lord, and the Lord wants to fill our bodies with Himself." 1Cor. 6:13b(TLB)

Sexual sin remains sexual sin, no matter how one may try to sugarcoat it. Premarital sex or fornication is wrong in every way alongside other sexual sins such as incest, sodomy, adultery, bestiality, necrophilia, homosexuality etc. The only Institution that validates sexual intercept is Biblical Marriage.

Every manufacturer has the terms and conditions related to his product documented which the consumer has to abide by to get the best out of the said product. The Same applies to the Lord God Almighty Himself. Elihu confronted Job with a critical question in that respect: "Just because you refuse to live on God's Terms, do you think He should start living on yours?" Job 34:33(The Message Bible) Everything concerning sex, including premarital sex, must be viewed from God's Vantage Point so that we may continue living on His Terms... Selah.

PRAYER:

Heavenly Father, we honour You for giving us the Biblical Boundaries which prevent the abuse of sexual intimacy. O Lord, we repent of every sin of fornication and ask You for the Grace to keep the marital bed undefiled in Jesus' Mighty Name. Amen.

# Chapter 20

Day 20: DAILY DEVOTIONAL
THE ADMINISTRATIVE MINISTRY

BIBLE READING: JEREMIAH 2:13; 1CORINTHIANS 12:4-6; MATTHEW 25:14-30; ACTS 6:1-6.
Now there are Diversities of Gifts, but the Same Spirit, and there are Differences of Administrations, but the Same Lord." 1Corinthians 12:4-5(KJV)

The Administrative Ministry is endowed with the Grace and Wisdom to structure the Church for productivity, growth and effectiveness in Ministry. However, the structure can become a limitation to the next level of growth if we are not flexible enough and learn when and how to always structure and re-structure when the need arises for continuous growth. (Lk. 5:38) This is because Church growth can pose more challenges and the need for periodic adjustments in our set structure. (Acts 6:1-6). Consequently, the only way to be more effective as a leader is to raise more capable hands to be able to take productivity to the next phase.

It is imperative to note that human beings are designed to create structures and systems which save us time, energy and resources as well as facilitate effectiveness in ministry. There are Three Basic Resources which must be managed in the area of Church administration:

1. Human Resources: This refers to souls that pass through the processes of Deliverance, Discipleship and Deployment into ministry. This area focuses on activities that we undertake to attract, develop and maintain an effective workforce.

2. Financial Resources: This refers to the management of money in the Church. Little can achieve much when there is prudence. In other words, there is financial wisdom involved in handling God's money.

3. Physical Resources: This refers to the Church facilities which is a key job description of Church administrators. Physical facilities have to be managed effectively because the environment affects productivity in both life and Ministry.

PRAYER:
Father, we thank You for the Grace and Wisdom in administering the Church of Jesus Christ for effectiveness and productivity in Jesus' Mighty Name. Amen.

# Chapter 21

Day 21: DAILY DEVOTIONAL
THE PURPOSE AND POWER OF FORGIVENESS

BIBLE READING: GENESIS 50:16-21; 2SAMUEL 16:5-13; MATTHEW 18:1-35
"Then Peter came to Him and said, “Lord, how often shall my brother sin against me, and I forgive him? Up to seven times?" Jesus said to him, "I do not say to you, up to seven times, but up to seventy times seven." Matthew 18: 21-22(NKJV)

Have you ever hurt somebody and wished to be forgiven? Do you spend time thinking about how someone has wronged you? How do you forgive? People through the ages have wrestled with similar questions. Jesus and Christianity have changed the world with the teachings of forgiveness. According to our main Scriptural Text, Jesus wasn't telling Peter to forgive someone 490 times and stop at 491. Rather, the numbers Jesus used were symbolic of infinity. We must forgive unconditionally and infinitely.

Let's further explore the power of forgiveness. To "forgive" means "to cease to feel resentment against; to pardon." (Webster).

It also means *"to harbour no grudge, bear no malice and to make peace." Whenever we forgive, we are being merciful, compassionate and humane. We are letting go of any grudges, removing focus from past mistakes or problems, dissolving any anger that we've been harbouring and being peacemakers.

The basic blessings of forgiveness include the following:
(a.) We gain a better view of ourselves and others that does not include resentment.
(b.) We start the healing process.

(c.) We feel happier because we are no longer angry.
(d.) We can move forward with a greater sense of freedom.
(e.) We provide others with the opportunity to change and grow.

Here are a few truths to remember about forgiving.

(1.) God forgave our sins...even the really bad ones: When we realize the Magnitude of a Perfect God knowing every one of our ugly, selfish, even horrible acts and thoughts yet still choosing to love and forgive us, it's so much easier to show mercy and forgiveness towards others. When you know God, your perspective and the very way you view life change. It's hard carrying a grudge when you're communicating daily with the God who gave His Son for you.

(2.) We might as well forgive because the offence will never cease: The fact that every person around us who doesn't know the Lord is lost, hurting and depraved pretty much guarantees there will be pain and offences in this life. (2Tim. 3:2) It's practically inevitable we will be hurt, attacked and offended by others before this life is over. Whether it's letting go of a co-worker insulting you, or something deeper, like a relationship wound, we're told to forgive, and let God deal with the offenders. Forgiving doesn't mean making light of wrongdoing, devaluing the hurt and pain we feel, or enabling the person who did wrong. But we are called to give our offences over to the Lord, completely, harbouring no ill-will towards our offenders.

(3.) Vengeance is the Lord's: Admittedly, some circumstances are more difficult to forgive than others. Instances of child abuse or infidelity can be some of the most difficult hurts to truly forgive. No matter the pain or heartache we are struggling with, it is important to remember no one cares more or is more upset about our pain than the Lord. If He loves us more than we even love our children, then He is even more offended and upset by wrongdoing against us. We should pray for our offenders to accept forgiveness, but if not, the Lord will deal with them in all his sovereignty someday. (Rom. 12:9) There's no pain or suffering we can't forgive, but we have to rely on God's power, not our own, and sincerely ask for his help. And when we genuinely forgive those who have hurt us, it draws us closer to God in a profoundly deep way. It's only when we align our thoughts and heart with God's Will for forgiveness that His Miraculous Healing will begin.

(4.) We have to forgive ourselves: If God, Who is sinless and without flaw, says we're forgiven, we need to believe it. I think many of us are held back in our Faith journey and even fail to fulfil our true destinies because we don't forgive ourselves for who we've been or the things we've done in the past.

The Bible says God holds no record of wrongs, yet how many times do those accusing thoughts pop into our minds reminding us of our failures and mistakes, to rob us of our joy and freedom? There is nothing we could do to hinder God's Forgiveness if we repent. (1Jn. 1:9) God used Paul, a Christian-killing Pharisee, to write most of the New Testament. Kind David had murder and adultery on his list of sins, but was eventually called a "man after God's Own Heart." What's important is Paul and David didn't look back, once forgiven. Now is the time to forgive yourself for everything and be joyful because God sees you as new.

(5.) Forgiveness leads to Freedom: Forgiving in sheer obedience to the Lord causes us to experience amazing power and freedom when we do. Bitterness is mental incarceration. There is so much weight, stress and exhaustion involved when you hold on to unforgiveness. Grudges weigh us down, deplete our energy and exercise unhealthy control over our lives. Forgiveness says to the offender, "I'm beyond your reach." What a profound truth! Forgiving someone is simply the act of setting a prisoner free only to discover that prisoner was you.

Here are some Basic Forgiveness-related Truths we need to know:

(i.) We have been forgiven: (Col. 2:13-15).
(ii.) Forgive because you've been forgiven: (Col. 3:13).
(iii.) Forgiveness restores broken relationships: (Gen. 50:17).
(iv.) Forgiveness is a Pathway to Love: (Lk. 7:47).
(v.) Forgiveness precedes healing (Lk. 5:17-26).
(vi.) God tells us to forgive instead of seeking revenge or bearing a grudge: (Lev. 19:18)

What is the proper procedure involved in forgiveness? Here are some basic tips for acceptable forgiveness:

(1.) Realize and admit your part in the conflict.
(2.) Ask Jesus, the Ultimate Forgiver, to empower you, remembering that He has forgiven you.
(3.) When you keep pain, bitterness and unforgiveness bottled up, it becomes a disease that may eventually kill you. You have to Let it go. Forgive the person that hurt you. Let go of the pain they caused you, the disappointment, the shame, regret, remorse etc. You can't keep that bottled up & fulfil your destiny.

PRAYER:
O Lord, please open my eyes to the Purpose and Power of Forgiveness. Lord, I receive grace to let go just as you have given us in your commandments in Jesus' mighty name Amen.

# Chapter 22

Day 22: DAILY DEVOTIONAL
BUILDING HIS CHURCH USING HIS METHODS

BIBLE READING: 1 PETER 2:4-10; EPHESIANS 2:18-22; 1CORINTHIANS 3:9-16; EPHESIANS. 4:11-13
"For he was [waiting expectantly and confidently] looking forward to the City which has Foundations, [an Eternal, Heavenly City] Whose Architect and Builder is God." Hebrews 11:10(AMP)

Our Anchor Scripture above reveals another Multidimensional Feature of God as an Architect and a Builder. A definition of these terms is fundamental to enhancing our understanding of these professional and practical skills which may corroborate the assertion that God is the First Architect and Builder. Cambridge dictionary defines an architect as “a person whose job is to design new buildings and make certain that they are built correctly” while Collins Dictionary defines a "Builder" as "a person whose job is to build or repair houses and other buildings." We are the Temple of God and He determines the design and builds us into a Spiritual House to offer spiritual Sacrifice: "You also, as living stones, are being built up a Spiritual House, a Holy Priesthood, to offer up Spiritual Sacrifices acceptable to God through Jesus Christ." 1Pet. 2:5(NKJV)

God is building a Spiritual House and Family which is the Dwelling Place for His Presence. It is noteworthy to know that we are a family fittingly joined together for a Holy Tabernacle for His Glory. (Eph. 2:21-22). The Building Material for this Spiritual House is human beings. Like the king commanded in the building of Solomon's temple, Jesus is commanding the

Church to go out there and gather these Precious Stones (souls) and prepare as well as place them where they belong in the House of God. This Building must be inspired by Revelation from God as evidenced in Jesus' Response to Peter: “Jesus answered and said to him, “Blessed are you, Simon Bar-Jonah, for flesh and blood has not revealed this to you, but My Father who is in Heaven. And I also say to you that you are Peter, and on this Rock, I will build My Church, and the gates of Hades shall not prevail against it.” Matt. 16:18(NKJV).

Paul the wise master builder admonished us on how to build in 1Corinthians 3:9-11:
” According to the Grace of God, which was given to me, as a wise master builder I have laid the Foundation, and another builds on it. But let each one take heed of how he builds on it. For no other foundation can anyone lay than that which is laid, which is Jesus Christ.” Jesus Christ is the

Foundation and Chief Cornerstone which has been laid for us. Everyone that builds must build according to God's Pattern documented in the Word of God because our Works will be tried with Fire to test if we will receive a reward: "Now if anyone builds on this foundation with gold, silver, precious stones, wood, hay, straw, each one's work will become clear; for the Day will declare it. After all, it will be revealed by Fire; and the Fire will test each one's work, of what sort it is. If anyone's work which he has built on it endures, he will receive a reward. If anyone's work is burned, he will suffer loss; but he will be saved, yet so as through fire." 1Cor.3:12-15(NKJV)

PRAYER:
Heavenly Father, I thank You for building Your Heavenly City where I will dwell with You and for building me into the Image of Christ as Your Temple where You will dwell. I will not defile this Temple You are building but will make it a place where You will be

pleased to dwell in Jesus' Mighty Name. Amen

# Chapter 23

Day 23: DAILY DEVOTIONAL
LOVE FOR THE BROTHERHOOD

BIBLE READING: JOHN 13:34-35; 1PETER 2:17; 1JOHN 3:14; 1 JOHN 4:20
"If anyone says “I love God,” but keeps on hating his brother, he is a liar; for if he doesn't love his brother who is right there in front of him, how can he love God Whom he has never seen?" 1John 4:20(The Living Bible)

Of the Three Cardinal Virtues according to the Scriptures, Agape Love remains the greatest for it is the Very Nature of the Lord God Almighty Himself. (1Cor. 13:13) You see, Faith may be the greatest force in the entire universe but Love is, without doubt, the Greatest Motive behind any thought, word or action. This is the reason the Subject of Agape Love in our Christian Faith can never be overemphasized. Since Love is the Acid Test of Genuine Christianity, the onus, therefore, lies upon us as true believers to love not just the Lord but also our fellow brethren. (1Jn. 3:16)

The Early Church was admonished to "Love the brotherhood." (1Pet. 2:17b) a phrase which was rendered in the Living Bible Translation as "Love Christians everywhere." This gives the genuine Christian believer the responsibility of loving the entire family of Christian believers without any reservation, denomination notwithstanding. In other words, anyone who worships the Lord in Spirit and Truth is a qualified member of the Fraternity of believers, (Jn. 4:23-24) hence we have a Divine Duty to love such as our covenant brothers. This was the Truth

Apostle Paul alluded to while praying for the Church in Ephesus: "For this reason, I bow my knees to the Father of our Lord Jesus Christ, From Whom the whole family in Heaven and Earth is named." (Eph. 3:14-15). Every single genuine believer, irrespective of denomination and interpretation of our Common Faith, is a bonafide family member of the Household of God, (Eph. 2:19) also known as the "Household of Faith." (Gal. 6:10b)

Each of us has a Divine Mandate rather than an option to love the brotherhood as members of the Christian Fraternity bound by the Blood Covenant as One Body in Christ. (1Cor. 12:12) let the Words of Jesus ring truer in the hearts of men and lead them lovingly to Him: "That they all may be one, as You, Father, are in Me, and I in You; that they may also be one in Us, that the world may believe that You sent Me." (Jn. 17:21)

PRAYER:

Heavenly Father, we magnify Your Holy Name. O Lord, please grant us a Revelation of the Christian Fraternity and enable us to always love the brotherhood in Jesus' Mighty Name. Amen.

# Chapter 24

Day 24: DAILY DEVOTIONAL
THE POWER OF THE ENVIRONMENT

MATTHEW 9:23-25; PSALM 1:1-4; PROVERBS 13:30; 1CORINTHIANS 15:33
And He cometh to Bethsaida, and they bring a blind man unto Him, and besought Him to touch him. And He took the blind man by the hand, and led him out of the town; and when He had spit on his eyes and put His Hands upon him, He asked him if he saw ought. And he looked up, and said, “I see men as trees, walking.” After that, He put His Hands again upon his eyes and made

him look up: and he was restored, and saw every man. And He sent him away to his house, saying, “Neither go into the town nor tell it to any in the town." Mark 8:22-26(KJV)

The environment can be defined as the surroundings or conditions in which a person, animal, plant or thing lives and operates. It contributes more than 50% of what determines the outcome, progress and survival of any individual, group or thing. It is the reason why certain plants cannot grow in certain locations; it is the reason why peer pressure is such a powerful thing for young people to deal with. It is the reason why children that grow up in certain families turn out in a particular way as compared with those that grow up in a different family setting.

The environment is so powerful that until you deal with the issue of the environment any effort you make otherwise will be fruitless and unproductive.

There are different types of environments:
(1.) Physical Environment.*
(2.) Spiritual Environment.
(3.) Social Environment.
(4.) Economic Environment.

Anything that exists creates an environment and also requires an environment to survive and thrive. The Bible warns us about the types of the social environment we should avoid. (Ps. 1:1-4, 1Cor. 15:33). These social environments mentioned in these Scriptures also create a spiritual environment that will harm our spiritual well-being.

This issue is so serious that the Lord God Almighty even warned Israel about their physical environment and why they should maintain proper hygiene and cleanliness as regards their excretory habits. (Deut. 23:12-14)

Jesus in His Earthly Ministry also understood the Power of the Environment. To be able to perform certain miracles and healings, He ensured He created the Right Spiritual Environment and avoided the wrong ones as can be seen in our main Bible passage above. If Jesus could pay attention to the Power of the Environment, who are we to treat it lightly? We must realize that destiny is location sensitive. You won't thrive in every environment, and certain supernatural manifestations would not be possible in some environments. (Mk. 6:2-5).

You must learn to obey promptly when the Spirit leads you to do something about your environment, whether it has to do with changing your friends, moving out of your family abode like in the case of Abraham, (Gen. 12:1) or staying in the location that God has called you to (like in the case of Jonah).

PRAYER:

Father, we pray that You give us an understanding of the role environment plays in our lives and walk with You. Please grant us the grace to always strive to maintain the right environments and avoid the wrong ones in Jesus' Name. Amen.

# Chapter 25

Day 25: DAILY DEVOTIONAL

THE PURPOSE AND POWER OF SMALL GROUPS

BIBLE READING: ACTS 2:42-47; LUKE 10:1-7; PSALM 133

Not forsaking the assembling of ourselves together, as is the manner of some, but exhorting one another, and so much the more as you see the Day approaching." Hebrews 10:25(NKJV)

The man was created by God as a relational being by nature who is dependent on Him and his environment. God by His Divine Providence set man in families for his wellbeing and harmonious coexistence: "God setteth the solitary in families...." (Ps. 68:6).

When you are born again, you automatically become a member of the Universal Church. However, God expects every believer to become first a member of a Local Church, especially for accountability and spiritual growth. (Heb. 13:17; Eph. 4:10-13) When you are baptized and committed to a Body of believers, you become a member of that Local Church.

Soul Winning, Consolidation, Discipleship and Commissioning of believers for the Work of the Ministry are the Core Purposes of a Local Church. One of the most effective ways to achieve this is through Small Groups which was a strategy the Early

Church deployed so effectively that within two years, they had disciplined the whole of Asia for Christ.

The Early Church had large meetings at the Synagogues, but they also met regularly in one another's houses. (Acts 2:42-46)

A Small Group is the Organization of members of a Local Church into smaller units for Worship, Soul Winning, Consolidation, Discipleship and Commissioning under the guidance of a Lay Leader. A Small Group system allows believers to participate in the Discovery Bible Study (DBS) where every member of the Small Group contributes to the discussion and asks questions under the guidance of a Lay Leader.

This Small Group is the fastest way of developing and multiplying disciples to fulfil the Great Commission.

The Vision of Jesus Christ is for everyone in the Body to be a fully mobilized disciple carrying the Presence and Power of God to their spheres of influence. Put succinctly, the Vision of Christ is Fourfold i.e., Win, Consolidate, Disciple and Send. An effective Small Group has proven to have the potential of rapidly multiplying the number of believers and Small Groups within a short time.

The Harvest is truly plentiful, and the labourers are few. (Matt. 9:37) The Power and Potential inherent in Small Groups when harnessed cannot be overemphasized because the spotlight is on everyone to evolve and manifest God's Inherent Gifts and Talents required for the Harvest. Since Labourers are few, Small Groups like regular Prayer meetings of a select few give the Holy Ghost a Platform to separate men: "While they were serving the Lord and fasting, the Holy Spirit said, "Set apart for Me Barnabas and Saul (Paul) for the work to which I have called them." (Acts 13:2).

PRAYER:
Father, I thank You for the Revelation of Small Groups, a Vital Strategy for this End Time Harvest. O Lord, please multiply Your Body as you did in the Early Church and now in a Greater Dimension in Jesus' Mighty Name. Amen.

# Chapter 26

*Day 26: DAILY DEVOTIONAL*
*THE MAKING OF THE MAN GOD USES*

*BIBLE VERSE: GALATIANS 4:1-2; DEUTERONOMY 8:2-3*
*"Then He commanded the multitudes to sit down on the grass. And He took the five loaves and the two fish and looked up to Heaven, He blessed and broke and gave the loaves to the disciples, and the disciples

gave to the multitudes." Matthew 14:19(NKJV).*

The Holy Scriptures emphasize to us that many are called but few are chosen. *(Matt. 20:16).* When it comes to Divine Calling, God calls everyone. In other words, everyone has a calling but when it comes to being chosen there is a price to pay for Divine Election.

You cannot be used by God the way you are hence there is the making of the man that God uses. If you will not allow God to work in you i.e., to prepare and mould you, then He cannot do much in, through and for you.

There are Four Major Processes involved in the making of the man whom God Will use:

*1.The Moulding/ Shaping of our Motives:* This is the heart of the entire matter. *(1 Sam. 16:7).* Your motive is your intention for doing something i.e., the reason for your actions. To God, the motive behind what we do either for Him or to our fellow human beings matters the most.

For example, the motive behind our giving, the services we render, our actions, the words we speak, our prayers etc., are critical because God does not start judging us from our actions but the motives of our hearts. He wants everything we do to be motivated by love because faith activates but love motivates. *(Gal. 5:6).*

*2. The Moulding of our Utterances:*
This is so key because our words are either constructive or destructive. *(Eph. 4:29).* Your utterances are the things that you say. God wants to shape our utterances so that when we open our mouths we will minister timely and edifying words loaded with grace to the hearers. *(Col. 4:6).*

*3. The Moulding/Shaping of our Attitudes:*

This is a major indicator of the source of one's confidence. *(Jer. 9:23-24).* Your attitude is the way you behave because of your feeling or opinion about something or someone. Your attitude determines your altitude in life. There are godly attitudes of the heart such as integrity, faithfulness, love and meekness (being gentle, teachable, malleable, instructable and correctable). Some people can neither be corrected nor instructed or taught because of pride.

*4. The Moulding of our Character/Values:* This is the Major Purpose of the Breaking Process. *(Matt. 14:14-21).* An unbroken vessel cannot carry the Glory of God. The Primary Purpose of the Wilderness Experience is to break us i.e., the pride in us, the rebellious tendencies in us, the greed and selfishness in us, etc., so that the Glory can be revealed through us to our generation. When God finishes with a man in the breaking process, all the arrogance, self-confidence and what one thinks he knows or can do will appear insignificant.

*PRAYER:*
My Lord God, please search my heart thoroughly. If there is any evil hidden motive of the heart, Precious Holy Spirit, please expose it. Change our hearts and make them ever true and acceptable before God in Jesus' Mighty Name. Amen.

# Chapter 27

Day 27: DAILY DEVOTIONAL
THE VALUE OF SPIRIT-CONTROLLED EMOTIONS

BIBLE READING: ISAIAH 12:3; EZEKIEL 3:14; GALATIANS 5:22-23
He continued, "Go home and prepare a feast, holiday food and drink; and share with those who don't have anything: This day is holy to God. Don't feel bad. The Joy of

God is your Strength!" Nehemiah 8:10(The Message Bible)

The Lord God Almighty designed man to be a social and relational being with inherent emotions. The Bible makes us understand that man is essentially a tripartite being i.e., he is a spirit possessing a soul and living in a body. (1Thess. 5:23) People act the way they do because they are spirits but rather because they have souls. In other words, our emotional expressions are primarily from our souls and not our spirits.

Just like the total man, the soul is also tripartite, having three dimensions:
(1.) The mind: This is the thinking faculty which is the base of reason. Simply put, the mind is the thinker of man. (Isa. 26:3)

(2.) The will: This is the decision-making faculty which is the base of choice. Simply put, the will is the choice of man. (Phil. 2:13)

(3.) The emotions: This is the sentimental faculty which is the base of feelings. Simply put, emotion is the feeler of man. (Ex. 32:19) This third dimension of the soul is the source of a diverse spectrum of the emotions we experience as human beings.

As stated earlier, man is a social and relational being who is designed for emotional bonding and interaction with others. It takes the Influence of the Holy Spirit to cultivate wholesome emotions hence the importance of true Christian believers to switch over to Spirit-controlled emotions. (Gal. 5:16) Negative emotions are overwhelmed by the Fruit of the Spirit which is powered by the Atmosphere of God's Presence.

One major distinction between the spirit and soul is that the former is the seat of man's identity while the latter is the seat of man's personality. In other words, what makes you a person is your HAVING a soul rather than your BEING a spirit. May we never forget that "God has not given us a spirit of fear but of Power and Love and a Sound Mind." (2Tim. 1:7)

PRAYER:
Heavenly Father, we magnify You for Who You are and for all You do for us. O Lord, please help us subdue and cultivate our emotions by the Unction and Power of the Holy Spirit in Jesus' Mighty Name. Amen.

# Chapter 28

Day 28: DAILY DEVOTIONAL
PRAY TO THE LORD OF THE HARVEST

BIBLE READING: MATTHEW 9:35-38; MARK 9:43,48; JOHN 4: 35-36; 1TIMOTHY 5:17-18
Then said He unto His disciples, "The Harvest truly is plenteous, but the labourers

are few. Pray ye, therefore, the Lord of the Harvest, that He will send forth labourers into His Harvest". Matthew 9:37-38(KJV)

Jesus admonishes all believers to be constantly aware that everyone lost has an Invaluable and Everlasting soul and must spend Eternity in Heaven or hell. The Truth is that many of them can be saved if only someone presents the Gospel to them. Hell in this passage refers to a place of Eternal Torment reserved for the ungodly alone. Mk. 9:43,48. The Bible teaches that one's existence does not end at death but continues forever, either in the Presence of God or in a place of punishment.

There are Four Things Jesus taught concerning the state of the lost:

1. Jesus teaches that there is a place of Eternal Punishment for those concerned before God: This is the terrifying reality of continuous punishment, the place of a "fire

that never shall be quenched." (Mk. 9:43), a place where for Eternity there would be "weeping and gnashing of teeth." (Matt. 13:42,50)

2. The Teachings of the Apostles speak about the Coming Judgment of God to inflict vengeance on those who disobey the Gospel: This refers to an Eternal Separation from the Presence of God. (2Thess. 1:5-9)

3. The Bible teaches that judgment on evildoers is certain: The main idea is condemnation, suffering, and separation
from God with no time limit. Christians may find this doctrine unpleasant or hard to understand. Yet we must submit to the Authority of God's Word and trust His Decision and Justice. (Heb. 9:27)

4. We must keep foremost in our thinking that God sent His Son to die so that no one needs to perish. It is not God's Intention or Desire to send anyone to hell. (2Pet. 3:9)

Those who enter hell do so by resisting the Salvation provided by God.

PRAYER:
Heavenly Father, please help us to proclaim and demonstrate the Good News of the Kingdom, to enable healing and empower people to experience dignity and fullness of life. Please help us to see people through Jesus' Eyes and to feel deep compassion for them in Jesus' Name. Amen.

www.ingramcontent.com/pod-product-compliance
Lightning Source LLC
LaVergne TN
LVHW050316160826
845677LV00014B/3425

* 9 7 9 8 3 5 2 7 5 6 1 3 3 *